IMAGINATION CELEBRATION

Written by Judy Leimbach and Joan Vydra

Illustrated by Elisa Ahl

Edited by Dianne Draze and Sonsie Conroy

ISBN 1-883055-05-9

Published by **Dandy Lion Publications**
    P.O. Box 190
    San Luis Obispo, CA 93406

Contents

Information for the Instructor

Why Teach Creative Thinking?

Educators are faced with the awesome challenge of preparing students for what they might encounter in the future. Adequate preparation for the future requires that children are able to use more than a one-solution thought process; more than the right-answer, convergent thinking required by many learning activities in our classrooms. The kinds of problems people will face in the future will require differentiated thinking. We cannot teach children all of the right answers, because at this point we don't know the questions let alone the answers. We can, however, provide our students with the skills needed to tackle the many problems that they will face. Creative thinking is one of the skills that will enable students to be successful problem solvers and life-long learners.

An emphasis on creative thinking skills in the classroom necessitates providing students with open-ended assignments and encouragement as they search for new answers. Unlike typical textbook questions that have a given right answer, creative questioning and thinking assumes that there may be one right answer, but there may also be many possibilities.

Students will not think creatively unless they are confronted with challenging tasks in an open, supportive environment. As students practice the many creative thinking tasks in this book, they will develop creative thinking skills, enabling them to become more capable and flexible learners, better prepared to handle future challenges.

About This Book

Imagination Celebration is specifically designed to be used in intermediate grades to develop several creative thinking skills. The first section of the book introduces the four cognitive creative skills first identified by Paul Torrance. Each of the four skills includes an explanation, a list of questions, and a list of tasks or activities that would require this behavior. The skill areas included are:

- **Fluency** - The ability to produce a large quantity of ideas.
- **Flexibility** - The ability to look at things from several different perspectives or viewpoints; to pursue different angles of thinking.
- **Originality** - The ability to produce new, novel, unique ideas.
- **Elaboration** - The ability to add on to an idea, to give details, to build groups of related ideas or to expand on ideas.

The next section includes reproducible worksheets that combine one or more of the separate cognitive areas. There are a variety of techniques that students will be exposed to as they work through these exercises. They will be asked to list ideas, use their imaginations, create analogies, think metaphorically, make unusual associations, and use attribute lists to create new ideas.

The final section is a list of projects that are presented as task cards. These projects are more long-term and extensive than the exercises that are presented on the worksheets. These tasks give students opportunities to use their creative abilities to plan fun, inventive projects.

Fluency

Fluent thinking is the mental flow of ideas and thoughts. It is the ability to produce a large quantity of creative ideas. Fluency activities may ask the learner to generate answers to questions of how many, what kinds, or what else. Fluent thinkers produce lots of ideas.

Fluency tasks cause a search through the learner's private collection or storehouse of knowledge and experiences for all possible responses. Brainstorming in small groups promotes fluency, as one person's idea triggers more responses from other members of the group. It's important in fluency exercises to withhold all judgments of right or wrong, appropriate or inappropriate, because attention is placed on quantity rather than the quality of the responses. This allows for an uninterrupted flow of thoughts and ideas and a search for all possibilities. The rationalization for promoting fluent thinking is that the more responses that are produced, the greater is the likelihood of producing an original idea or of producing a satisfactory solution. If you have twenty ideas to choose from, you have a greater probability of having a quality idea within that group than if you have only two ideas.

A teacher encourages fluent thinking every time he or she asks:

1. How many _____ can you think of?

2. In what ways might we _____?

3. What are all the ways you could _____?

4. Make a long list of things that _____.

5. How many different examples (reasons, solutions, etc.) can you think of?

6. How many ways can you think of to _____?

7. What are all the things that are _____?

8. What comes to mind when you think of _____?

9. How long a list can you make?

Fluency Tasks

Make a long list of:

- ways to get from one place to another
- things you can catch
- things you could say or do to thank another person
- words that mean "watch"
- things that crash
- reasons not to smoke
- names for an ice cream shop
- things to do with a potato
- things that are soft, but strong
- titles for a TV sitcom about your school
- ways to save paper
- similes for "as fast as..." or "as slow as..."
- examples of animals helping people
- names for a class or school newsletter
- things that close
- words that could create a mood of excitement
- things underground
- things that have bumps on them
- things that are symmetrical
- ways to hold things together
- everything that comes to mind when you think of a dozen
- excuses for not doing homework
- uses for a single wheel
- invisible things
- ways to save energy
- ways to be kind to someone
- uses for a pile of cardboard
- titles for a book about magnets
- ways to make spelling fun
- things that mean love
- things that melt
- things to do with a rubber raft
- words that make you think of fun
- things that sparkle
- things that have a cord

Note: For your convenience, the following page has been included to use with these fluency tasks.

Brainstorming

Brainstorming is thinking of a lot of ideas. You shouldn't stop to judge whether the ideas are good or bad; you just write down as many ideas as you can.

Use this topic for brainstorming. Write as many ideas as you can.

Make a long list of _____

_____   _____

_____   _____

_____   _____

_____   _____

_____   _____

_____   _____

_____   _____

_____   _____

_____   _____

_____   _____

_____   _____

_____   _____

Flexibility

Flexible thinking extends fluent thinking. Flexibility results in many different kinds of ideas. It is the ability to look at things from different angles, see the situation from several perspectives. It is the ability to shift trains of thought and produce a variety of ideas. The flexible thinker produces original ideas by forcing associations not usually thought of in a given context. A student who thinks flexibly often redefines mental sets by viewing things from other perspectives. The flexible thinker responds well to the questions, "What else is possible?" or "What is another way of looking at this?"

For example, if asked in what ways an empty paper towel tube could be used, a flexible response might be to use it as a measure for spaghetti or as a tunnel for ants. When asked what one dangling earring could be used for, the flexible thinker might suggest using it as a chandelier in a doll house or as a fishing lure. The flexible thinker will be able to produce a variety of ideas. From this ability to see things from many different angles comes the ability to produce a larger quantity of ideas (fluency) and more unique ideas (originality).

The purpose of flexible thinking is to generate and promote responses that deviate from the normal thought patterns. Flexibility allows for invention and the discovery of new or untested ideas. Flexible thinkers see things in different ways and can find uses for almost anything. This shift in direction and perspective comes through the breaking of mindsets, the brave world of the flexible thinker.

Questions to encourage flexible thinking include:

1. Can you think of a different way to _____?

2. What else might be happening?

3. What other things are possible?

4. What are some different ways to look at this?

5. How would _____ look at this?

6. What are some different reasons for _____?

7. What if _____?

8. What ideas can you get about _____ by thinking about _____?

9. _____ is to _____ as _____ is to _____. (analogy)

10. What else could you use _____ for?

11. What relationship can you think of between _____ and _____?

12. In what ways are the following two unlike objects alike?

Flexibility Tasks

1. Which would you rather be? Why?
   - a piano or a telephone?
   - a tree or a diamond?
   - a race car or a river?
   - a computer or a painting?

2. Think of ways the following unlike things are alike:
   - a banana and a snake
   - a chair and a tree
   - a teacup and a telephone
   - a pencil and a plant

3. Write six sentences using the word "spring" in different ways.

4. Make a shape that is strong, a shape that is weak, a shape that is happy, a shape that is sad, a shape that is angry, and a shape that is contented.

5. How might these people view "charge" differently?

a teenager	an electrician	a criminal
a rock star	a ticket agent	a knight

   Can you think of other contexts for this word?

6. Describe a fur as seen by a trapper, a furrier, an animal rights activist.

7. If you could go back in time, what period of history would you return to? What do you think your life would be like?

8. Make a drawing with no people that shows anger, joy or love.

9. Choose a fairy tale and rewrite it from another character's perspective.

10. Discuss traffic from the following perspectives:

pedestrians	drivers
business owners	city planners

11. List all the things that come to mind when you think of nature. Group your ideas in two different ways.

12. What if babies inherited knowledge and were born already knowing everything their parents know? Describe both the good and the bad effects.

13. What if we got all of our nutrition through pills and didn't need food? What might be good about this? What might be bad?

14. Discuss two different points of view on the following topics:

traffic accidents	dress codes
school lunch programs	Native American burial sites

15. Imagine changing places with a famous person. Who would you choose? How would your life be different?

16. Discuss skate boarding from the perspective of the following people:

youngster	parent	doctor
school principal	manufacturer of skateboards	

Originality

Originality is the creative thinking behavior that produces new or novel responses. Originality is often the by-product of other creative thinking behaviors. For example, when working through a fluency exercise some learners will produce ideas not thought of by anyone else. The more ideas that are produced (fluency), and the more they depart from the norm (flexibility), the better are the chances that there will be original responses. In a flexibility exercise, some learners will produce novel ideas as a result of thinking about the situation from different perspectives. These unique responses are examples of originality.

The most original idea can be the first one generated or it can be the one that comes when learners are pushed for one last response. Original responses might come in tandem with fluent thinking, elaboration, flexibility, or perseverance; or possibly in combination with several of these creative thinking processes. The more teachers stress creativity and divergent thinking, the greater the likelihood of original responses. Students will learn to value original thinking when teachers provide activities that facilitate original responses and also accept and recognize original thinking. Since original ideas may be distinct departures from the norms, the instructor must blend tolerance and open-mindedness with the ability to evaluate whether the idea not only stands out from the ordinary, but also meets the stated criteria.

A teacher can encourage students to be original by asking, "What else, or what more?" These questions, designed to promote fluent thinking, let students know that we want them to stretch their minds even more. Originality will happen in most classrooms where teachers show they value original thought.

Other questions and statements to elicit original thinking include:

1. What is a new, original way to _____?
2. How could you make it different?
3. What can you think of that no one else will think of?
4. Can you invent a new _____?
5. How can you change _____ to make _____?
6. How can you combine _____ and _____ to make something new?
7. How can you combine _____ and _____ to solve the problem of _____?
8. Devise a new way to _____.
9. Create an ideal _____ for a _____.

Originality Tasks

1. Invent your own number system.

2. Create your own recipe for peace.

3. Design a flow chart that shows the way to lasting friendship.

4. Make up nonsense words and write interesting definitions for them.

5. Imagine you are interviewing a football. Think of original questions to ask, then make up interesting answers for them.

6. Design a fashionable outfit for the year 2075.

7. Invent a new game using cards and dice.

8. Draw the design for a "Rube Goldberg" invention to _____.

9. Use word puns to write riddles.

     Example: What do cats like for dessert? (mice cream)

10. Draw a maze that has only one solution.

11. Create a new superhero with unique powers.

12. Write a limerick about a fairy tale or nursery rhyme character.

13. Design a book jacket for a book you would like to write.

14. Create a remedy for greed.

15. Write your initials on a piece of paper, then use them to create a picture.

16. Create your own cartoon.

17. Write original similes for "as strong as...", "as gullible as...", "as fierce as...", "as gentle as...", "as original as..."

18. Design a modern-day coach for Cinderella.

19. Create a conversation between two lockers

Elaboration

Elaboration is the creative thinking behavior that results in adding to or embellishing an idea. It is the ability to add details, fill in the gaps, build groups of related ideas and expand ideas. By adding onto a drawing, a sentence, a thought, or a story, the learner is making it a more complete, more interesting finished product. The purpose of elaboration is to expand or stretch; to add to the original idea.

Elaboration is a creative thinking skill because the learner is required to ask more questions and seek more answers than are generally given or to take a simple idea and develop a more complex thought. Students elaborate when they change a simple sentence like "The dog ran" into a more complex sentence like "The mangy brown dog ran quickly away from the mischievous group of young boys." It is also elaboration (and originality) when a simple doodle is made from letters or lines. The more the learner elaborates on the original drawing, the more complex and creative the doodle becomes.

A teacher has students elaborate every time he or she asks a question like:

1. What else can you tell me about _____?
2. Can you be more descriptive?
3. What can you add to make it more interesting or complete?
4. Using these guidelines, what can you develop?
5. Using these basic elements, what can you create?
6. How can you complete this?
7. What could be added to _____ to improve it?
8. What new ideas can you add?
9. Can you add supportive information?

Elaboration Tasks

1. Add details to make a basic drawing more interesting.

2. Add phrases to make short sentences more descriptive.

3. Give your opinion on a particular topic. Add information to support your opinion.

4. The invention of _____ changed people's lives. Explain how. Give examples.

5. Print your first, middle, and last names on a sheet of paper. Make a crossword puzzle by adding words that describe you.

6. Choose a children's game and add ideas that will make it more fun or challenging.

7. Complete this sentence: "Doubts, like fear,..." Elaborate on your idea to write a poem about doubts.

8. Choose a theme for a party. Plan a party around that theme. Include details like invitations, decorations, table settings, entertainment and prizes.

9. Given the outline of a mountain range, draw in details to bring the scene to life.

10. Given a basic car design, what options would you add to make a super luxury car?

11. List words that describe summer; then write a poem about summer.

12. Give examples to explain the saying "Every cloud has a silver lining."

13. Write an editorial article with the headline "It Is Time to Elect a Woman President."

14. Given a basic recipe, add ingredients that will make it taste even better.

15. What things could be added to improve a school bus or to adapt it to another use?

16. Write another verse for a poem or nursery rhyme.

17. If you could make any additions you wanted to your house or yard, what would you add?

18. List three adjectives that describe a friend. Use them to write a paragraph about this friend.

19. Cut a 2-inch square out of a magazine picture and glue it to a sheet of paper. Exchange papers with a partner. Complete the picture you were given by adding details that extend the picture.

20. Write another chapter for a favorite book.

Blocks to Creativity

One of the reasons we are not more creative is our unwillingness to break the rules we set for ourselves or our tendency to do things the same way all the time. We tend to do things the same old way each day. Here is a list of some things that you could do that would add variety to your day and help you break out of your usual mindset and look at things in a different way. Choose at least two of these things to do. Tell what differences you noticed or what insights you had as a result of this different experience.

☐ Take a new path to school.

☐ Ride an elevator facing the back of the elevator instead of the front.

☐ Read a new type of book.

☐ Eat a food you've never tried before.

☐ Put on your clothes in a different order than you usually do.

☐ Play with different people at recess.

☐ Explore a new place.

☐ Imagine something you have never actually experienced before.

☐ Listen with an open mind to a point of view that is different than yours.

I noticed _____

_____

_____

_____

Metaphors

A metaphor makes a comparison between two things. Put on your thinking cap and try to complete the following metaphors in creative ways.

Our classroom is like a Sega game because_____

_____

Geography is like a Concorde jet because _____

_____

Homework is like a ball-point pen because _____

_____

Our school is like a garden because _____

_____

My teacher is like an atlas because_____

_____

Our school is like a mall because _____

_____

Our classroom is like a _____ because _____

_____

Our school is like a_____ because _____

_____

More Metaphors

Think of creative connections and list as many ideas as you can.

1. How is an apple like a new idea?

The core provides the seeds for more ideas.

_____   _____

_____   _____

_____   _____

_____   _____

2. How is school like a factory?

It works best when we all do our part.   _____

_____   _____

_____   _____

_____   _____

_____   _____

3. How is a paper clip like a dream?

_____   _____

_____   _____

_____   _____

_____   _____

4. How is a worn out shoe like a young puppy?

_____   _____

_____   _____

_____   _____

Comparisons

In what ways is a dream like a sandwich?

_____

_____

_____

_____

_____

In what ways is a forest like a football?

_____

_____

_____

_____

In what ways is an airplane like an acrobat?

_____

_____

_____

_____

A Rose Is Like...

List things (other than flowers) that are like a rose in some way. Think of different types of similarities.

_____   _____

_____   _____

_____   _____

_____   _____

_____   _____

_____   _____

Personal Metaphors

In this exercise, you will compare yourself to things in nature.
Name three ways you are like a tree.

_____

_____

_____

_____

Think of different ways you are like each of these things.

a river - _____

a mountain - _____

a meadow - _____

a storm - _____

an ocean - _____

a flower - _____

a drop of rain - _____

a snowflake - _____

Listing Pairs

What are all the things in nature you can think of that come in pairs?

_____   _____

_____   _____

_____   _____

_____   _____

_____   _____

Feeling Poems

An interesting way to describe a feeling is by using your senses. Imagine what color the feeling would be and how it would taste, smell, sound, and feel.

For example:

Anger is fiery red.

It tastes like jalapeño peppers stinging my tongue.

It smells like the smoldering embers of a forest fire.

If sounds like dynamite blasting craters in the earth.

It feels like a volcano rumbling inside me.

Choose a different feeling. Use the format above to write a poem about that feeling.

_____

_____

_____

_____

_____

_____

_____

_____

Drawing Feelings

Make a shape that is tenderness.

Make a shape that is frustration.

Problem-Solving Analogies

An analogy is the comparison between things that may be similar in only some respects. Analogies can be used to solve problems. First, the problem is stated. Then analogies are created that are similar to the original problem. One or more of the analogies is solved. Finally, the solutions are transferred from the analogy to the original problem. Here's an example:

1. The Problem: *Students cheat on exams.*

2. Analogies: *People take things from stores.*
Pets get on the furniture when you're not looking.
Squirrels eat the birds' food.

3. Analogy Solutions:

How to stop people from taking things from stores:

- *put up video surveillance*

- *attach electronic anti-theft tags to merchandise*

- *have more security people patrol the aisles*

- *establish tough penalties for shoplifters*

How to stop pets from getting on the furniture:

- cover the furniture with sheets of plastic

- keep the pets in other rooms when you're away

- punish the pets when found on the furniture

How to stop squirrels from eating the birds' food:

- put baffles on the bird feeders

- give the squirrels other food sources

- put bird food in weight-activated bird feeders

4. Transfer the solutions :

- put up video surveillance

- have teachers walk the aisles

- establish tough penalties for cheaters

- put up carrels on student desks

- separate desks during test taking

- give alternative test forms

Problem-Solving Analogies

Choose one of the following problems. Then using the example on page 21, create analogies that are like the situation, solve one or two of the analogies and then transfer the solutions to the problem.

Problems:

(circle your choice)

- A personal problem of your choice
- Students leave garbage on the school yard
- Your new puppy cries all night and keeps everyone awake
- You want to join the baseball team but you're not very good at throwing or hitting

Create the analogies

1. _____

2. _____

3. _____

Solve the analogies _____

_____

_____

_____

_____

_____

_____

_____

_____

Transfer the solutions

_____

_____

_____

Creative Comparisons

Draw a line from each word on the left to a word on the right. Then list at least two different ways these two things are alike.

car   pencil

house   telephone

tree   vacuum

neon sign   daffodil

Paired words   **Similarities**

_____

_____

_____

_____

Which One?

Which is sharper — a smile or a frown? Why? _____

_____

Which is more colorful — hate or love? Why? _____

_____

Which is colder — the future or the past? Why? _____

_____

Inventing New Options

One of the ways that inventors come up with new ideas for new products is by asking themselves questions such as:

1. What else can this be used for?
2. What could be substituted?
3. How could this be modified?
4. How could this be combined with something else?
5. What if this were larger or smaller?
6. How could this be rearranged in some way?
7. What could be added?

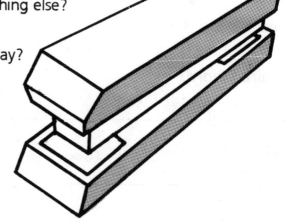

Think of a stapler. Invent new and improved options for the stapler by completing the questions below. Think of several ideas for each question.

What else can this be used for? _____

_____

What could be substituted? _____

_____

How could this be modified? _____

_____

How could this be combined with something else? _____

_____

What if this were made larger or smaller? _____

_____

How could this be rearranged in some way? _____

_____

What could be added? _____

_____

Choose another item in your classroom and use these questions to help you think of ways that you could either improve it or modify it for another use.

Parodies

A parody is a literary or musical composition imitating the characteristic style of some other work in a nonsensical manner. Parodies are fun to write, read, or sing. An example of a parody of "The Night Before Christmas" might begin:

'Twas the night before Halloween
    and all through the school,
Not a creature was stirring,
    not even a ghoul.
The principal's office was locked up tight.
There was just one custodian on duty that night.

Complete this parody, or choose a different song or poem and write a parody of your own.

_____

_____

_____

_____

_____

_____

_____

_____

_____

_____

_____

_____

_____

_____

_____

Word Play

The way that letters, symbols, or words are arranged can suggest longer, complete phrases. For example, you might represent the phrase "read between the lines" as

lines read lines or ||| **read**|||

Write or draw a representation of each of the following phrases.

1. scrambled eggs

2. square meal

3. 90° angle

4. fat chance

5. double trouble

6. shot in the dark

Think of four more phrases and then draw a graphic representation of each phrase. Have a friend guess what the drawings represent.

7.

8.

9.

10.

Reasoning Why

Choose three of the following situations and for each situation, give at least five good reasons why this might be happening.

- John didn't have his homework done on time
- Your alarm clock didn't go off
- A television program's rating suddenly dropped
- You went to bed at 4 o'clock in the afternoon
- A person suddenly stops eating candy
- The teacher walked out of the classroom

Situation _____

_____

_____

_____

_____

_____

Situation _____

_____

_____

_____

_____

_____

Situation _____

_____

_____

_____

_____

_____

A Slew of Solutions

When we have a problem, the more solutions we can think of, the better chance we have of solving the problem. Look at these two problems and think of things you might do in each situation. List as many different ideas as you can.

You're at school and **you** tear your pants.

_____

_____

_____

_____

_____

_____

_____

You want a computer **game** that costs $50.00, and you have only $15.00.

_____

_____

_____

_____

_____

_____

_____

_____

Put a * next to the **three** ideas in each list that you **think** are your best ideas.

Sense Imaginations

Write thoughtful, creative answers
to these questions.

What does gentle look like? _____

_____

What does yellow smell like? _____

_____

What does soft taste like? _____

_____

What does green sound like? _____

_____

Listing

Make a list of things that are:

soft and white

_____

_____

_____

_____

_____

_____

durable and round

_____

_____

_____

_____

_____

_____

Shipshape Ideas

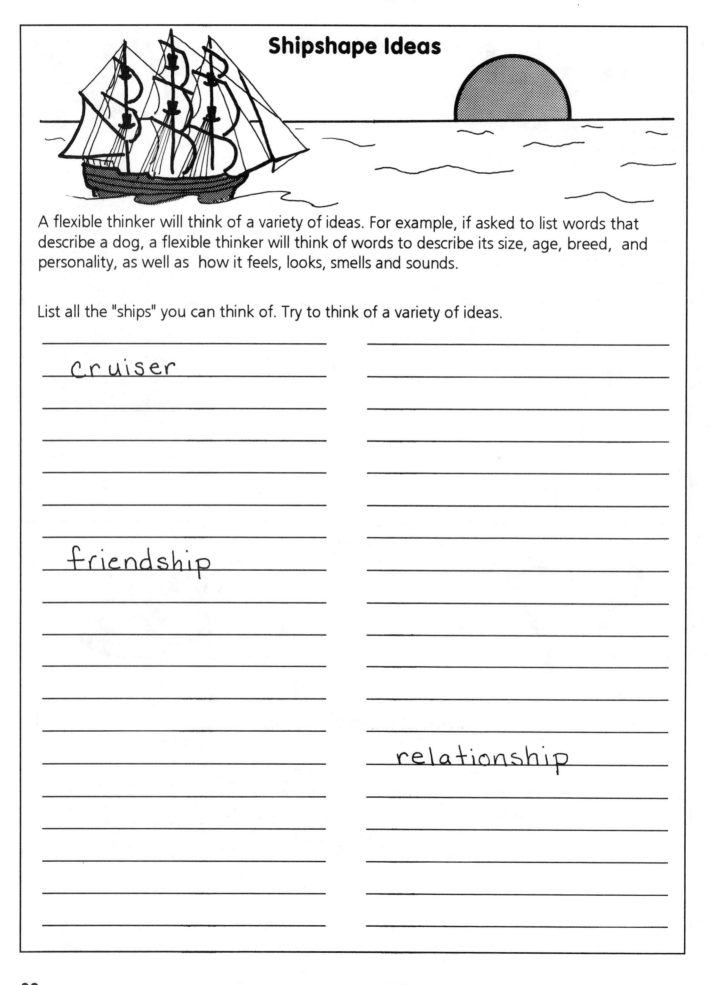

A flexible thinker will think of a variety of ideas. For example, if asked to list words that describe a dog, a flexible thinker will think of words to describe its size, age, breed, and personality, as well as how it feels, looks, smells and sounds.

List all the "ships" you can think of. Try to think of a variety of ideas.

cruiser

friendship

relationship

Combining Words

Write eight different sentences using the words in the lists below. Use at least one word from each list in every sentence. Use each word in lists A and D in two different sentences. Use each word in lists B and C in only one sentence.

A	B	C	D
tiger	glamorous	wearily	student
acrobat	wicked	gladly	bone
teacher	skinny	silently	mouse
dog	quiet	swiftly	clown
	brave	loudly	
	polite	lazily	
	shaggy	shyly	
	kind	softly	

1. _____

2. _____

3. _____

4. _____

5. _____

6. _____

7. _____

8. _____

Animal Combination

What if you combined an elephant, a giraffe, and a turtle? Name and describe your new animal. Draw a picture on the back of this paper.

_____   _____

_____   _____

_____   _____

Other Uses

Paper clips are used for holding things together. Think of several other things you could do with a paper clip.

_____

_____

_____

_____

_____

_____

_____

_____

_____

_____

Rulers are used to measure. Think of several uses for a ruler besides being used to measure something.

_____

_____

_____

_____

_____

_____

_____

_____

_____

_____

Choose **an object in your desk**. Think of several uses for the object besides its usual use.

_____

_____

_____

_____

_____

_____

_____

_____

_____

_____

Point of View

Put yourself in the place of one of the following inanimate objects. Imagine what life would be like as that object. Imagine how you would feel and what you might think or say (if you could think or speak). Write a paragraph about life from the point of view of the object.

lounge chair   old shoe   stuffed toy

fountain   football   feather

_____

_____

_____

_____

_____

_____

_____

_____

_____

_____

Thinking Like a Vegetable

Be your least favorite vegetable. Make a list of arguments to present to other vegetables to convince them to let you into their exclusive "Good Vegetable Club."

_____   _____

_____   _____

_____   _____

_____   _____

Creative Jigsaw Puzzle

Directions for the Teacher:

Flexible thinking requires breaking mind sets. The puzzle below is unlike most jigsaw puzzles because the "corner" pieces fit together in the middle of the puzzle. Use the following directions to prepare the puzzle for students.

- Duplicate copies of the puzzle on this page on sturdy paper like tag board.
- Cut out the pieces of each individual puzzle and place them in an envelope.
- Divide the class into small groups of 3 - 5.
- Give each group an envelope with the puzzle pieces.
- Ask each group to put the puzzle together. Do not give them any information about how the finished puzzle will look.

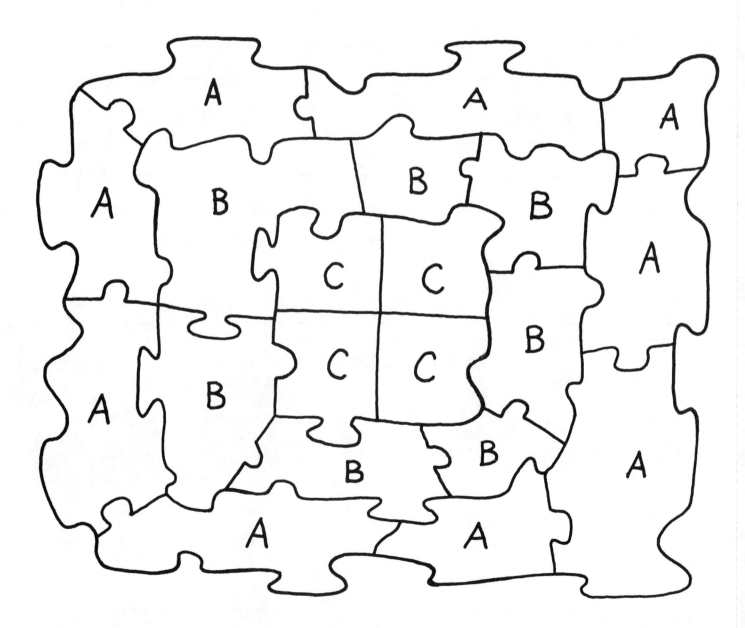

Different Perspectives

Use the circles below to make pictures of things from either a bird's eye view (looking down on) or a bug's eye view (looking up at). Put captions on your pictures.

Examples:

A bird's eye view of a person in a wide brim hat.

A bug's eye view of a rocket lifting off into space.

A Soaring Challenge

Your challenge is to soar by thinking of at least ten four-word questions in which the words begin with the letters **W, I, N** and **G** (in that order). Make each sentence a different word pattern.

Example - **W**here **i**s **N**ed's **g**ift?

_____

_____

_____

_____

_____

_____

_____

_____

_____

_____

Imagine Flying

Imagine that you had wings and could soar through the air. Describe how it would feel. Draw a picture on another piece of paper of what you would see.

_____

_____

_____

Sentence Challenges

Write five sentences in which each new word of the
sentence begins with the last letter of the word that
precedes it. Each sentence must have at least four
words.

Example: Three eels slid down near Ron.

1. _____
2. _____
3. _____
4. _____
5. _____

Write three sentences in which each word of the sentence begins with the last two letters
of the word that precedes it.

Example: Two women entertained Edna.

1. _____
2. _____
3. _____

Word Patterns

Use your creative thinking skills to detect the pattern in this list
of words. Add words to the list that will continue the pattern.

1. envelope
2. eleven
3. towel
4. potato

5. _____
6. _____
7. _____
8. _____

9. _____
10. _____
11. _____
12. _____

The Problem Solving Tree

You have discovered a tree that can grow anything you want. Choose two of the following problems and then complete the trees to illustrate what you will grow on the trees to accomplish each goal. Finally, choose one tree and explain how you will use what you've grown to accomplish the given goal.

Goals: end homelessness   end violence   obtain world peace   solve the drug problem

Beneath the Sea

Complete the story below with your own original twist. Try to think of a story line that will be different from those of your classmates.

The scuba diver approached the shiny bucket with caution. An odd glow seemed to emanate from the bucket's metallic finish, and yet the bucket looked empty.

_____

_____

_____

_____

_____

_____

_____

_____

_____

_____

_____

Continue on the back of this sheet or on another piece of paper.

In Your Own Words

A publishing company has supplied you with the following words and asked you to create definitions. Using standard dictionary format, create definitions for each of the words. At least one word should have dual usage; for instance, as a verb and a noun. At least one word should be a noun, one an adjective, and one a verb. Make up two of your own words and the dictionary listing for each one.

jambast - _____

_____

smitz - _____

_____

isty - _____

_____

imbic - _____

_____

quamp - _____

_____

histip - _____

_____

_____

_____

_____

Descriptive Sentences

Add descriptive words and phrases to make each of the following sentences more interesting.

Example: *The witch stirred her brew.*

In her dark cave one Halloween night, the ugly witch cackled wickedly as she stirred her evil brew.

1. Waves splashed upon the shore. _____

_____

2. The carolers sang in the moonlight. _____

_____

3. The lion prowled. _____

_____

4. The river overflowed its banks. _____

_____

Memorable Menus

You're having a dinner party and here's your guest list. What will you serve for dinner that will please each of the guests? Make a menu on another piece of paper.

- a majestic mauve monster
- a quite quintessential queen
- the wild west wind
- noble Mother Nature
- a likable lady lion
- a slightly silly skua

Making Words

Add additional letters to letters **N, D** and **S** to make words. You can add letters before, after or between the letters **N, D** and **S**.

Examples:

ba<u>nds</u>   wi<u>nds</u>urfing   <u>needs</u>   ca<u>ndies</u>

_____   _____

_____   _____

_____   _____

_____   _____

_____   _____

_____   _____

_____   _____

Imperfections

What are some things that are better (or more beautiful) because of their imperfections?

_____

_____

_____

_____

_____   _____

_____   _____

_____   <u>the oyster's pearl</u>

_____   _____

_____   _____

Complete the Picture

Complete a picture using all of the lines on this page. You may turn the paper any way that is helpful to you. Add many details to make your drawing interesting. When you are finished, write a title for your completed picture.

A Good Beginning

Combine the two phrases in each box and add other words and phrases to make the opening sentence for an interesting story. Do this for all five boxes. Then pick your favorite opening sentence and complete the story on another piece of paper.

leaping frogs   **in the boat**

_____

_____

shiny windows   **trick or treat**

_____

_____

crackling fire   **inside the tent**

_____

_____

car horn   **noisy party**

_____

_____

carton of milk   **black and white spotted cow**

_____

_____

Expressing Thoughts

Write interesting, descriptive endings for these sentences. Let the elaborative details paint a clear picture of how you think about things.

1. The environment, like a sea shell, _____

2. Leaders, like teachers, should _____

3. Democracy, like a chocolate chip cookie, _____

4. Prejudice, like an animal, _____

5. Tragedy moves like _____

6. Happiness, like a crystal, _____

7. I am like a _____ _____ because _____

    _____

8. The future, like a book on the shelf, _____

9. Cruelty, like friendliness, _____

The Shape and Feel of Things

Draw a shape that is hurt feelings.

Find something the texture of kindness and glue it here.

Drawing Ideas

There is an old saying that says "a picture is worth a thousand words." Add the details that are needed to make this dragon a part of a story without words. Place him in an unusual setting. Write a title for the picture.

Making Pictures

Below are some meaningless shapes. Add the details necessary to make something unique out of each shape. Give each drawing a title.

'Tis the Season!

Choose at least two items from the list below and draw them into this winter picture. On another sheet of paper write a story with all of the details needed to make the scene plausible.

blooming apple tree	sand castle	fireworks
beach ball	baseball bat	tulips in bloom
squirrel gathering nuts	a grill	beach umbrella

Ode to a Computer

On a separate sheet of paper list at least 30 words you associate with computers. Use that list to write an acrostic poem by starting each line of the poem with the letters in the word computer.

C _____

O _____

M _____

P _____

U _____

T _____

E _____

R _____

Happiness Is...

Write a recipe for happiness from the perspective of someone either younger or older than you are.

_____

_____   _____

_____   _____

_____   _____

_____   _____

_____   _____

_____   _____

Changing Sentences

Add adjectives, verbs, nouns, and adverbs that begin with the given letters to complete the following sentences.

1. The c_____ boy ran through the meadow c_____.

2. The e_____ boy ran through the meadow e_____.

3. The f_____ boy ran through the meadow f_____.

4. The h_____ boy ran through the meadow h_____.

5. The c_____ waves c_____ upon the shore.

6. The p_____ waves p_____ upon the shore.

7. The s_____ waves s_____ upon the shore.

8. The r_____ waves r_____ upon the shore.

9. The c_____ dog barked c_____ at the c_____.

10. The d_____ dog barked d_____ at the d_____.

11. The h_____ dog barked h_____ at the h_____.

12. The s_____ dog barked s_____ at the s_____.

New Words

Invent words to describe the following things.

smell of fresh grass - _____   taste of burnt cookies - _____

flight of a bird - _____   sound of falling snow - _____

feeling of erasers - _____   warmth of a fire - _____

What If?

Choose one of these "what if?" situations. Think of
as many possible consequences or effects as you
can. After you have made a long list, choose
several of your best ideas and present them in a
story, a poem or a skit.

- What if glass conducted electricity?
- What if you always knew what other people were feeling?
- What if all food tasted like apples?
- What if people didn't like the taste of sugar until the age of 18?

Ant Brigade

What if you could train ants? What are all the things you could use them for?

Sandwich Sampler

As the new owner of Sam's Super Sandwiches, you want to invent new sandwiches that will give your customers several choices for lunch time fare. Use the following lines to list several possible choices for bread, filling, spread, and extras.

bread	filling	spread	extras

Use the ideas you have listed to make new sandwich combinations. Name each sandwich and describe its ingredients.

A Better Box

How could you make the standard lunch box better? List ideas for each of the components of a lunch box. Then combine the ideas into a new improved version.

shape	material	decoration	handle

Draw and label your lunch box.

Candy Creator

Complete the following lists of characteristics of candy bars. List several different possibilities for each attribute.

filling	coating	shape	other features
_____	_____	_____	_____
_____	_____	_____	_____
_____	_____	_____	_____
_____	_____	_____	_____
_____	_____	_____	_____
_____	_____	_____	_____
_____	_____	_____	_____
_____	_____	_____	_____

Combine the ideas to make a new candy bar. Name your candy. Describe it.

_____

_____

_____

Draw a package or advertisement for your new candy bar.

Colorful Thoughts

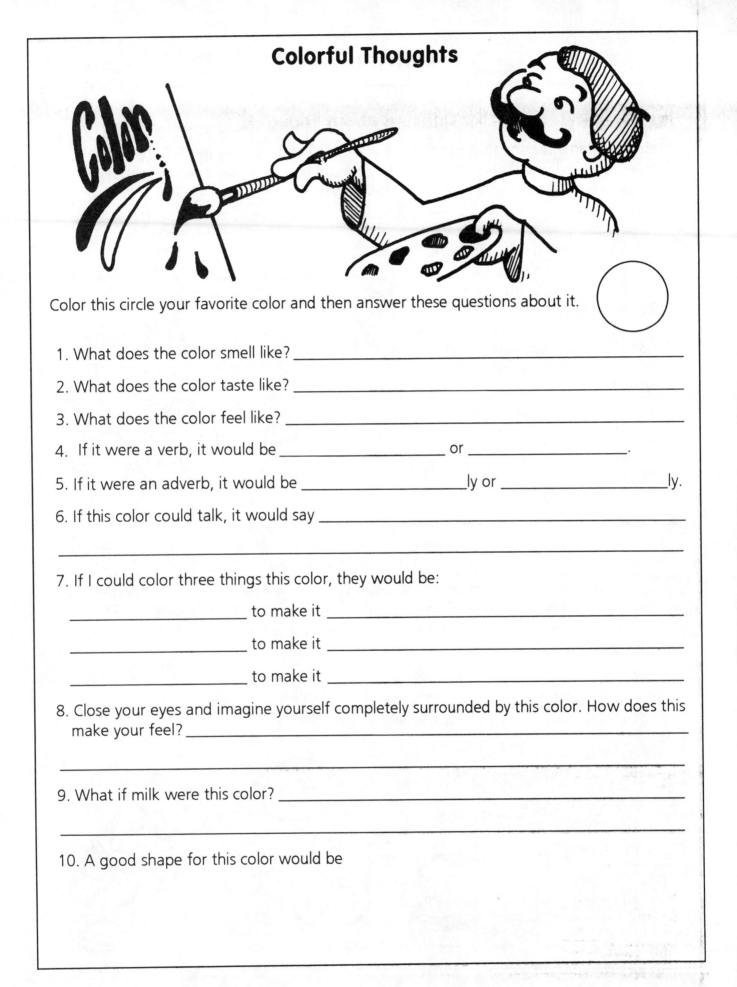

Color this circle your favorite color and then answer these questions about it.

1. What does the color smell like? _____

2. What does the color taste like? _____

3. What does the color feel like? _____

4. If it were a verb, it would be _____ or _____.

5. If it were an adverb, it would be _____ly or _____ly.

6. If this color could talk, it would say _____

_____

7. If I could color three things this color, they would be:

_____ to make it _____

_____ to make it _____

_____ to make it _____

8. Close your eyes and imagine yourself completely surrounded by this color. How does this make your feel? _____

_____

9. What if milk were this color? _____

_____

10. A good shape for this color would be

Creativity Projects

Thinking About Thoughts

Thinking is an interesting subject to think about! What are thoughts? Where do they come from? Do you control them? Do they control you? Make a list of metaphors and similes to describe thoughts in several different ways.

For example, one student described his thoughts like this: "My thoughts are like a car on an icy road, sometimes I can control them and sometimes I can't."

Present your ideas as a webbing, a written essay or a collage of words and pictures.

Start a Business

Imagine you are starting a chain of restaurants. You have found that many successful restaurants are popular because they appeal to children. You have decided that if you can make your restaurant a place where kids really want to go, your business will be highly successful.

Think about what things would make your restaurant appeal to young people. Think about a theme for it, how it would be decorated, what type of food would be served, and what gimmicks you might use to attract customers.

Make a presentation that includes:

- the name of the restaurant
- the theme
- why it would appeal to young people
- the logo
- a floor plan
- a menu

Creativity Projects

A New Game

You have a 10 m. by 20 m. court, a paddle for every two players, a nerf ball and four wastebaskets. Make a new game using this equipment.

Editorial Cartoon

An editorial cartoon makes a comment on a subject of public interest. These cartoons often use symbolism to represent countries or issues. They often use caricatures to depict public figures. You can find examples on the editorial pages of the newspaper.

Choose a set of characters from a nursery rhyme or fairy tale. Choose a current national or local problem. Pair the characters with the problem and create an editorial cartoon. Draw your cartoon and add captions.

Creativity Projects

Wanted Poster

Wanted posters of criminals who have either eluded capture, escaped from prison, or are suspected of a major crime hang in post offices all over the country. These posters include a picture of the criminal , vital statistics that include height, weight, hair color, and distinguishing marks, and a list of crimes for which the subject is wanted. Complete the profile drawings of the subjects below and then write the details necessary to complete the poster.

Ima Suspect   Ivor Doneit

Mack T. Knife   Brute Force

Choose your best character profile and do a full-size poster.

Symbolic Nursery Rhyme

Here is the story of Little Miss Muffet told in symbolic form. Think of ideas for showing a different nursery rhyme using symbols. Put each line of the nursery rhyme on a separate piece of paper and staple the pages together to make a book.

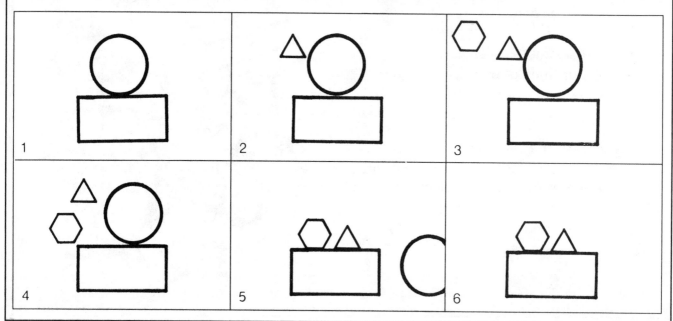

Creativity Projects

Your Own Island

In the last several years major cruise lines have purchased uninhabited Caribbean Islands and created ports of call that include areas for snorkeling, scuba diving, sailing, tanning, swimming, eating, drinking, and jet skiing. If you owned a cruise line and could purchase an island, what would you name the island? Draw the island on another piece of paper and label each of the attractions and activity locations. Give each area a creative name.

Note: The Caribbean is much clamer and safer for water activities than the Atlantic Ocean.

Beach Business

You are the owner of a company that designs and manufactures beach wear.

Make up a name and logo for your company.

Design at least two of the following:

- shark-proof swimwear
- the perfect beach shoe
- clothing that is cool but prevents sunburn
- a towel for toddlers
- a hat that has specific characteristics that will make it useful for the beach

Creativity Projects

Classroom Modifications

Find two things in your classroom that are not designed for use by people with limited physical abilities. Draw and describe what kind of modifications you would make that would make these items easier to use.

Marketing a New Product

You have been hired to come up with a name for a new toothpaste and a design for a container that will appeal to a wide variety of consumers. Make an outline of a toothpaste container and then fill in the details for the front and back of this new product. Write a jingle to advertise your new toothpaste.

60

Creativity Projects

Concept Collage

Choose one of these topics and make a collage of words and pictures to represent it. Try to show the concept without using the actual word.

- serenity
- youth
- chaos
- freedom
- beauty

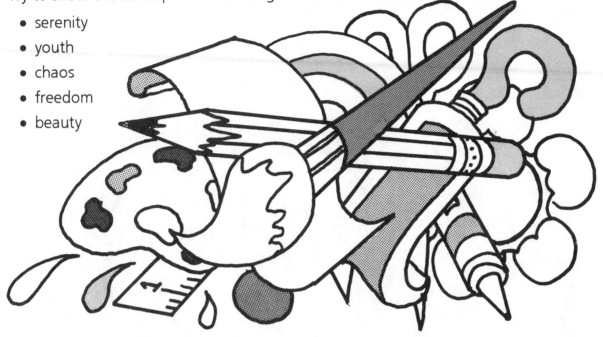

A Perfect Pencil

Imagine what an electric pencil might be like. Draw the inside and describe the special features of this new invention.

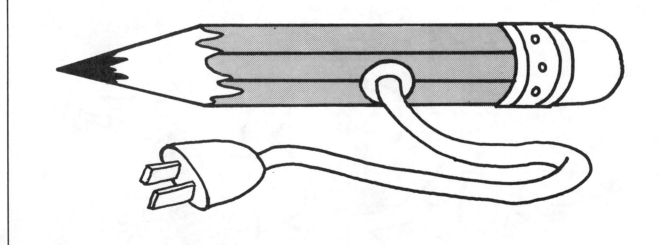

Creativity Projects

Opposites Poem

Choose two of these opposing word pairs or select your own pair of antonyms. Write a poem that creates a bridge between the two words.

love - hate   sparkling - dull

preserve - destroy   genuine - imitation

multicolored - monotone   peaceful - warring

A Personal Cause

Choose a special cause that you feel strongly about. Think of creative ways that you could raise support for this cause or inform other people about it. Make a **poster**, a **skit**, or a **pamphlet** that will illustrate the problem and will convince other people to join you in supporting this cause.

Creativity Projects

Movement

Think about how you can use your body creatively to communicate ideas to other people. Choose a feeling (joy, frustration, terror, etc.) or a concept (peace, chaos, freedom, etc.) that you want to communicate. Then plan and perform a series of movements that will communicate this concept to your audience. You may wish to select music or sounds to accompany your performance.

Recreational Park

Plan a new recreational park for your area that would attract people from other parts of your state. Make a **technical description** of the park in drawing and writing. Write a **speech** to convince people in your area to support the park. Make a **brochure** to attract travelers to the area.

Creativity Projects

Ring-a-Ling

We have telephones that ring, buzz, talk to computers, transmit written messages, and take messages. It's hard to imagine any more improvements for a telephone, but surely you can think of some. What else would you like a telephone to do? Make a list of improvements. Combine the best ideas into your improved model. Make a picture and label the important features.

Recyclables

Find something that would normally be thrown away, like a styrofoam food container, a plastic bag, an egg carton, etc. Make one of the following things out of this object.

- an animal home
- way to attract insects
- something to be used in a car
- a device for categorizing something
- something a skateboarder would want